GENESIS:
The Beginnings

A 4-week course to help junior highers understand how learning from the past can help them be better Christians today

by Norman D. Stolpe

Group®
Loveland, Colorado

Genesis: The Beginnings
Copyright © 1991 by Group Publishing, Inc.

First Printing

Credits
Edited by Stephen Parolini
Cover designed by Jill Bendykowski and DeWain Stoll
Interior designed by Jan Aufdemberge and Judy Atwood Bienick
Illustrations by Judy Atwood Bienick

ISBN 1-55945-111-4
Printed in the United States of America

CONTENTS

Genesis: The Beginnings

The Creation: in God's Image

Help junior highers understand God's Creation and the significance of being created in God's image.

The Fall: It's So Tempting

Help junior highers recognize and resist temptation.

Giving Your Best

Help junior highers learn what it means to give their best to God.

The Flood: God to the Rescue

Help junior highers trust God to rescue them from difficult situations.

GENESIS: THE BEGINNINGS

"I'm worthless. Why'd God create me in the first place?"

"I could figure out all the answers, but I save time if I look at someone else's paper. I only do it once in a while. There's nothing wrong with cheating a little bit, is there?"

"Sometimes when I mess up, I figure God doesn't want anything to do with me. Am I right?"

• • •

Where can you turn to help kids answer these serious questions?

How about beginning with page one of your Bible. Yes, the book of Genesis.

While they've probably already heard the familiar stories—Creation, Adam and Eve, Cain and Abel, and Noah and the Flood—junior highers and middle schoolers may not understand how each of these stories is relevant to their lives.

The book of Genesis is filled with insightful stories of God's relationship with his people. And each story is a terrific way to bring hope and insight into a junior higher's pressure-filled and unsure world.

Junior Highers' Top Pressures

● 65 percent feel "a lot" of pressure to earn money.

● 69 percent feel "a lot" of pressure to prepare for the future.

● 83 percent feel "a lot" of pressure to do well in school.

Many teenagers feel unworthy or inadequate because of the pressures they face. By seeing how God created each person in his own image in the creation story, kids can begin to renew their sense of worth—and accept the challenge to live like Jesus.

By understanding Adam and Eve's story—kids can understand how temptation happens to everyone. And by learning about Jesus' victory over sin, they can understand how to resist temptation.

Upon first reading, Genesis may seem like a depressing book. It chronicles many times when people broke their relationship with God. And it depicts God's often-severe responses to people's sins. But beyond the stories of a world falling apart are wonderful lessons on the beauty of God's best creation— people. And there are great stories of God's steadfast love. And stories of God's hope for a repaired relationship with his people.

Genesis: The Beginnings takes your junior highers and middle schoolers behind the scenes in Genesis—to discover that their own relationships with God are mirrored in the familiar stories there. Junior highers need a message of hope. This course will take kids on a journey of hopefulness through the beginnings of God's relationship with his creation. Familiar stories will ring with new meaning as kids dive into creative learning experiences.

COURSE OBJECTIVES

By the end of this course your students will:
- identify qualities in themselves that show how they're made in God's image;
- recognize their importance in God's creation;
- explore biblical accounts of people who wrestled with temptation;
- develop a specific plan to resist temptation;
- discover what it means to give God your best;
- learn to trust God to help them in difficult situations; and
- explore Noah's faith as a model to live by.

HOW TO USE THIS COURSE

ACTIVE LEARNING

Think back on an important lesson you've learned in life. Did you learn it from reading about it? from hearing about it? from something you experienced? Chances are, the most important lessons you've learned came from something you experienced. That's what active learning is—learning by doing. And active learning is a key element in Group's Active Bible Curriculum.

Active learning leads students in doing things that help them understand important principles, messages and ideas. It's a discovery process that helps kids internalize what they learn.

Each lesson section in Group's Active Bible Curriculum plays an important part in active learning:

The **Opener** involves kids in the topic in fun and unusual ways.

The **Action and Reflection** includes an experience designed to evoke specific feelings in the students. This section also processes those feelings through "How did you feel?" questions and applies the message to situations kids face.

The **Bible Application** actively connects the topic with the Bible. It helps kids see how the Bible is relevant to the situations they face.

The **Commitment** helps students internalize the Bible's message and commit to make changes in their lives.

The **Closing** funnels the lesson's message into a time of creative reflection and prayer.

When you put all the sections together, you get a lesson that's fun to teach—and kids get messages they'll remember.

BEFORE THE 4-WEEK SESSION

● Read the Introduction, the Course Objectives and This Course at a Glance.

● Decide how you'll publicize the course using the art on the Publicity Page (p. 9). Prepare fliers, newsletter articles and posters as needed.

● Look at the Bonus Ideas (p. 45) and decide which ones you'll use.

• Read the opening statements, Objectives and Bible Basis for the lesson. The Bible Basis shows how specific passages relate to junior highers and middle schoolers today.

• Choose which Opener and Closing options to use. Each is appropriate for a different kind of group. The first option is often more active.

• Gather necessary supplies from This Lesson at a Glance.

• Read each section of the lesson. Adjust where necessary for your class size and meeting room.

BEFORE EACH LESSON

• The approximate minutes listed give you an idea of how long each activity will take. Each lesson is designed to take 35 to 60 minutes. Shorten or lengthen activities as needed to fit your group.

• If you see you're going to have extra time, do an activity or two from the "If You Still Have Time . . . " box or from the Bonus Ideas (p. 45).

• Dive into the activities with the kids. Don't be a spectator. The lesson will be more successful and rewarding to both you and your students.

HELPFUL HINTS

• The answers given after discussion questions are responses your students *might* give. They aren't the only answers or the "right" answers. If needed, use them to spark discussion. Kids won't always say what you wish they'd say. That's why some of the responses given are negative or controversial. If someone responds negatively, don't be shocked. Accept the person, and use the opportunity to explore other angles of the issue.

THIS COURSE AT A GLANCE

Before you dive into the lessons, familiarize yourself with each lesson aim. Then read the scripture passages.
- Study them as a background to the lessons.
- Use them as a basis for your personal devotions.
- Think about how they relate to kids' circumstances today.

LESSON 1: THE CREATION: IN GOD'S IMAGE
Lesson Aim: To help junior highers understand God's Creation and the significance of being created in God's image.
Bible Basis: Genesis 1:1—2:25 and Ephesians 4:13.

LESSON 2: THE FALL: IT'S SO TEMPTING
Lesson Aim: To help junior highers recognize and resist temptation.
Bible Basis: Genesis 3:1-24 and 1 Corinthians 10:13.

LESSON 3: GIVING YOUR BEST
Lesson Aim: To help junior highers learn what it means to give their best to God.
Bible Basis: Genesis 4:1-15 and Matthew 6:33.

LESSON 4: THE FLOOD: GOD TO THE RESCUE
Lesson Aim: To help junior highers trust God to rescue them from difficult situations.
Bible Basis: Genesis 6:1—9:29 and Hebrews 11:7.

PUBLICITY PAGE

Grab your junior highers' attention! Copy this page, then cut and paste the art of your choice in your church bulletin or newsletter to advertise this course on Genesis. Or copy and use the ready-made flier as a bulletin insert. Permission to photocopy clip art is granted for local church use.

Splash this art on posters, fliers or even postcards! Just add the vital details: the date and time the course begins, and where you'll meet.

It's that simple.

Come to _____

On _____

At _____

Come learn how to boost your self-image, deal with temptation and improve your relationship with God as Genesis comes to life with creative activities and discussions.

Genesis: The Beginnings

THE CREATION: IN GOD'S IMAGE

Junior highers hear conflicting arguments about the creation of the world. From school they may hear one thing. From parents or church they may hear another. Kids need to see beyond the controversy to the key ingredient of creation—that they were created in God's image.

To help junior highers understand God's creation and the significance of being created in God's image.

Students will:
● recognize their importance in God's creation;
● discuss the important issues in thinking about God's creation;
● learn what it means to be created in God's image; and
● identify qualities in each other that show how they're made in God's image.

Look up the following scriptures. Then read the background paragraphs to see how the passages relate to your junior highers and middle schoolers.

Genesis 1:1—2:25 describes the creation of the universe. The word "genesis" means origin. The most obvious origins recorded in this book include the origin of the world, man and woman, and civilization. But even more important than the origin of these things is the purpose behind creation.

Junior highers and middle schoolers may be confused by the creation vs. evolution controversy and miss the message of the Bible's creation account. Kids need to understand that God has a good purpose for creation and they're an important part of that purpose.

In **Ephesians 4:13**, Paul writes that the goal of Christian growth is to be conformed to Jesus' image.

The general theme of Ephesians is establishing God's purpose for the church. This brief passage identifies an important goal for Christians—to be like Jesus.

Being conformed to Jesus' image is an overwhelming concept. Kids may not be able to comprehend the importance of that idea. But they can see how Jesus lived his life—and model their lives after his example.

THIS LESSON AT A GLANCE

Section	Minutes	What Students Will Do	Supplies
Opener (Option 1)	up to 5	**My Sculpture**—Create sculptures that show their inner qualities.	Soft modeling compound or clay
(Option 2)		**Speed Draw**—Guess words from the creation story as volunteers draw them.	Newsprint, markers, paper, candy or gum
Action and Reflection	15 to 20	**Creation Debate**—Debate issues relating to creation and talk about the importance of being created in God's image.	"Creation Debate" handouts (p. 18), Bibles, paper, pencils
Bible Application	10 to 15	**Same and Different**—List ways that people are similar to and different from God.	"Same and Different" handouts (p. 19), Bibles, pencils
Commitment	5 to 10	**Strength Bombardment**—Tell others how they see God's image in them.	Four balls or knotted rags
Closing (Option 1)	5 to 10	**Picture Show**—Create a short slide show presenting the wonder of God's creation.	Slide projector, nature slides, slide tray, hymnal, background music (optional)
(Option 2)		**Sing Praises**—Write new words to a familiar hymn or song, praising God's creation.	Paper, pencils, hymnal

The Lesson

OPENER
(up to 5 minutes)

☐ OPTION 1: MY SCULPTURE

Give kids each soft modeling compound or clay. Say: **Out of this clay, we're each going to create something new and meaningful. In three minutes form your clay into a shape that represents one or more of your positive inner qualities. If you're a patient person, you might form the clay into a clock without hands to represent patience. If you're a loving person, you might form a heart to repre-**

sent love. Choose a quality you know describes you well.

After kids complete their sculptures, have them each explain their sculpture. Then ask:

● **How'd you feel as you created something out of clay?** (I enjoyed it; it was difficult to think of what to create.)

● **Was it easy to create something that represented a positive quality you have? Why or why not?** (Yes, I know my best qualities; no, I couldn't think of a quality to sculpt.)

● **Which aspect of this activity is more important: that you created something or the quality you represented in your creation? Explain.** (The creation, it's not every day you get to create something; the quality, people are more important than things.)

Say: **Today we're going to explore the topic of creation as recorded in the book of Genesis. We'll take a hard look at the controversy surrounding the issue, and learn what's really important for us to know about creation.**

☐ OPTION 2: SPEED DRAW

Form teams of no more than five. Have teams each find a place in the room away from the other teams. Give teams each newsprint and markers. Have one person from each team come up to you. Show each contestant the first word on the "Game Words" list in the margin (cover the rest with a sheet of paper).

Have the contestants each run back to their team and draw pictures depicting the word you just showed them. Tell the artists not to talk, or write letters, numbers or symbols. When someone in each team guesses the word exactly, he or she must come back to you and tell you the word. Then show that person the next word for his or her team in the "Game Words" list. Remember to keep the other words covered so kids don't see what's coming up.

Continue the game until one team has completed all the words. Give members of that team each a prize of candy or a pack of gum.

Ask:

● **How'd you feel as you participated in this game?** (Nervous; I enjoyed it; confused.)

● **Was it easy to create pictures representing the various words? Explain.** (Some were easy because they were things; some were difficult because they weren't objects.)

Say: **You may have noticed a theme in the words you were trying to draw and guess. This theme, creation, is the focus of our first lesson in this course. Just as you tried to figure out the drawings, many people try to figure out how the world was created. Today we'll explore what's really important for us to know about creation.**

Game Words

Light
Heavens
Life
Created
Multiply
Good
Seas
Image
Breath
Garden

ACTION AND REFLECTION

(15 to 20 minutes)

CREATION DEBATE

Have kids line up according to the time they got out of bed this morning—from earliest to latest. Have kids count off by fours to create four teams. Assign an area of the room to each team. Give groups each one section of the "Creation Debate" handout (p. 18), a Bible, paper and pencils.

Say: **Read your section of the "Creation Debate" handout I just gave you. This describes how you'll approach the issue of creation in a debate we'll start in just a few minutes. Talk about how you'll act in the debate, based on the instructions on your handout. You can use the suggested scripture passages to support your position.**

Allow four minutes for kids to read and discuss the handout. Then have kids set up their chairs in one square, with each team sitting on one side of the square. Allow teams each one minute to present their position. Then tell teams they can challenge things the other teams said.

Form a circle, and ask:

● **How'd you feel when you presented your position?** (Confident; uncomfortable; anxious.)

● **After the teams presented their positions, did you feel swayed to any one position? Explain.** (Yes, I liked what was said about God's purpose; no, they all seemed weak.)

● **How'd you feel when everyone started talking at once during the debate?** (Embarrassed; anxious; I didn't like it.)

● **How was this activity like the way some people approach the issue of creation vs. evolution?** (People don't listen to others; people have different views.)

● **What'd you learn about the creation debate from this activity?** (It's a losing battle; it's hard to convince people of what you believe.)

● **Which position did you agree with most? Explain.**

Say: **From this activity we can learn that arguing about creation and evolution doesn't accomplish anything. When we get caught up in the creation debate, we lose sight of the fact that we were created in God's image.**

At this point in the lesson, you might want to present your church's position on creation. Talk with your senior pastor to find out what you should tell kids.

Ask:

● **How does it make you feel, knowing you were created in God's image?** (It's scary; I'm honored.) Kids may feel uncomfortable answering this question. Kids might say things such as "God must be funny-looking" or "I feel sorry for God." If they do, use that opportunity to talk about how God sees each person as important and worthwhile—no matter what we see as our faults. Be sensitive to kids who feel they're ugly or who have difficulty relating to other kids.

Say: **Being created in God's image means we're like him in many ways. But we're also different from him.**

SAME AND DIFFERENT

Form groups of no more than three. Give groups each a "Same and Different" handout (p. 19), a Bible and a pencil. Have groups each complete their handout. Then have groups each share how they completed their handout.

Ask:

● **We're created in God's image. What does that mean?** Note: This is a tough question for kids. You might want to have a senior pastor talk briefly with kids about your church's approach to this question.

● **What makes humans unique?** (The ability to think; our ability to love others.)

● **What can you learn from the passages you read that will affect the way you live each day as a Christian?** (I'll be aware of God's presence; I'll try to live like God wants.)

Say: **It's overwhelming to think that we were created in God's image. And it's tough to always work toward living as Jesus did. But each of us has at least one quality that matches how God would want us to live. Let's have some fun as we celebrate God's best creations—us!**

STRENGTH BOMBARDMENT

Have kids stand and form a square as they did in chairs for the Creation Debate activity. Give one person on each of the four sides a ball (or a knotted rag). Say: **Earlier when you were in this square, you debated about how the world was created. But now, as you look around, think about the wonderful purpose God has for each one of you.**

On "go," say one way you see God reflected in a particular person here. For example, you might say "I see God reflected in you because you're kind to others." Then call out that person's name and toss him or her the ball. Be ready, there are four balls and they may come to you at any time. Be sure everyone gets tossed a ball at least once. The positive things you say will help build strength in the person you say them about.

Allow three to five minutes for kids to toss the balls and tell ways they see God reflected in each other.

Then ask:

● **What can we do in our lives to better reflect the image of God in us?** (Be creative; be responsible.)

Have kids each tell one thing they'll do to better reflect God's image. Then form a circle, and have kids put their arms around each other for a group hug.

BIBLE APPLICATION
(10 to 15 minutes)

COMMITMENT
(5 to 10 minutes)

Table Talk

The Table Talk activity in this course helps junior highers and their parents discuss relevant stories from the book of Genesis.

If you choose to use the Table Talk activity, this is a good time to show students the "Table Talk" handout (p. 20). Ask them to spend time with their parents completing it.

Before kids leave, give them each the "Table Talk" handout to take home, or tell them you'll be sending it to their parents.

Or use the Table Talk idea found in the Bonus Ideas (p. 45) for a meeting based on the handout.

CLOSING
(5 to 10 minutes)

☐ OPTION 1: PICTURE SHOW

Set up the slide projector. Have kids each quickly choose a nature slide they like. Place slides in a slide tray, and have kids each keep track of when their slide will appear.

When the slides are ready, have kids sing "All Creatures of Our God and King" or another familiar hymn. Or have background music playing. As each slide is shown, have the person who picked that slide say one thing he or she appreciates about God's creation. Then, after all the slides have been shown, have kids stand one at a time in front of the projector. For each person, have everyone say in unison: **Thank you Lord for creating (name).**

Have kids close with a moment of silent prayer.

☐ OPTION 2: SING PRAISES

Have kids choose a familiar hymn or song they enjoy singing. Then form groups of no more than four, and have kids each write a new verse for that song which describes the wonder of God's creation. Have hymnals available so kids can match words to the song.

Allow five minutes for groups to write their verses. Then form a circle and have kids each say one thing they like about being created in God's image. Close by having groups each sing their verse of the song.

If You Still Have Time . . .

Portrait of God—Give kids paper and pencils, and have them draw a "portrait" of God. Encourage kids to draw pictures that represent the qualities God has shared with us by making us in his image. For example, kids might draw images representing compassion, love and mercy.

Creation Celebration—Form groups of no more than four. Allow a few minutes for groups each to create a four-line poem or cheer about God's creation. Then have groups recite their poems or do their cheers one after the other as a celebration of God's creation.

Contract
AND READING GUIDE

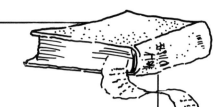

Contract

I believe that reading the Bible is an important part of my faith development. I hereby agree to read through the entire book of Genesis during the next four weeks. I further agree to faithfully attend all the class sessions on *Genesis: The Beginnings* and, inasmuch as I am able, support and encourage others to read this book.

Signed _____   Date _____

Reading Guide

The following outline is designed to help you read through the book of Genesis in four weeks.

Segment	Passage	Title
☐ 1	Genesis 1:1—2:25	The Beginning
☐ 2	Genesis 3:1-24	Sin Begins
☐ 3	Genesis 4:1-26	First Family
☐ 4	Genesis 5:1—6:8	Adam's Family Tree
☐ 5	Genesis 6:9—7:24	And the Rains Came . . .
☐ 6	Genesis 8:1—9:29	All Dried Up
☐ 7	Genesis 10:1—11:32	Nations Grow and Spread
☐ 8	Genesis 12:1—14:24	Abram and Lot
☐ 9	Genesis 15:1—16:16	Many Descendants
☐ 10	Genesis 17:1-27	The Promised Son
☐ 11	Genesis 18:1—19:38	Turning to Salt
☐ 12	Genesis 20:1-18	Trickery
☐ 13	Genesis 21:1—23:20	God Provides
☐ 14	Genesis 24:1-67	A New Wife for Isaac
☐ 15	Genesis 25:1—26:35	Expensive Soup for Esau
☐ 16	Genesis 27:1-40	Hairy Trick
☐ 17	Genesis 27:41—28:22	Jacob's Dream
☐ 18	Genesis 29:1—30:43	The Trick's on Jacob
☐ 19	Genesis 31:1-55	Running Away
☐ 20	Genesis 32:1—33:20	Wrestling With God
☐ 21	Genesis 34:1—36:43	Israel's Family
☐ 22	Genesis 37:1—39:23	Joseph's Trials
☐ 23	Genesis 40:1—41:57	Telling Dreams
☐ 24	Genesis 42:1—43:34	When Dreams Come True
☐ 25	Genesis 44:1—45:28	A Trap Is Set
☐ 26	Genesis 46:1—47:12	Jacob Goes to Egypt
☐ 27	Genesis 47:13—49:28	Blessings
☐ 28	Genesis 49:29—50:26	Jacob and Joseph Die

CREATION
DEBATE

Cut apart these four position cards and give one to each group.

• • • • • • • • • • • • • • • Scientific Study Group • • • • • • • • • • • • • • •

Your group doesn't see what religion has to do with the beginning of the world. You believe only science can measure and study physical things. You say things such as "Since we can't go back to the beginning of time, there's no way to know what God did or didn't do. All we know is what we can prove today."

During your position statement, refer to the Bible as a "good book" with interesting stories but not a useful tool for scientific study. Try to convince the other groups that science is the only way to define the origin of the world. Suggest evolution as the only possible answer for the origin of humanity.

When the time comes to challenge other groups, have all group members begin talking at once, trying to convince the other groups you're right. Stir up the other groups by talking all at once and pointing out the holes in their positions.

• • • • • • • • • • • • • • • • Divine Design Group • • • • • • • • • • • • • • • •

Your group readily admits that the Bible isn't a science manual. You want others to understand that the importance of the Bible story of creation is the message it brings to Christians.

In your position statement say things such as "What's important about creation isn't the process, but the purpose." Try to convince people that creation couldn't have happened by chance, suggesting that God must've been in charge. Talk about how our lives have meaning because of the plan God set up in creation. Refer to Genesis 1:27-28 about God having made man and woman in his image. Say: "Being created in God's image is the important message of creation—not whether it took a million years or a day."

When the time comes to challenge other groups, have all group members begin talking at once, trying to convince the other groups you're right. Stir up the other groups by talking all at once and pointing out the holes in their positions.

• • • • • • • • • • • • • • • Believable Bible Group • • • • • • • • • • • • • • •

You believe that the Bible is an exact record of the beginning of the world. When Genesis refers to a "day" you believe it means one 24-hour day. You have no doubt that God created the world and that he did so as described in Genesis.

In your position statement, try to convince others that the only way to truly understand creation is to read the Bible account. You believe the scientific approach doesn't allow for God's great power. Refer to specific Bible verses in Genesis 1—2 as you describe how you think the world was created.

When the time comes to challenge other groups, have all group members begin talking at once, trying to convince the other groups you're right. Stir up the other groups by talking all at once and pointing out the holes in their positions.

• • • • • • • • • • • • • • • Concerned Christian Group • • • • • • • • • • • • • • •

You're hesitant to criticize the scientific group for their methods. You believe science and religion can work together to describe the origin of the world. You believe it's possible that the world was created as the scientist group describes, but you believe God must have had a hand in the process—whatever it was.

In your position statement, try to convince the other groups that science will only support the fact that we have a wonderful creator.

When the time comes to challenge other groups, have all group members begin talking at once, trying to convince the other groups you're right. Stir up the other groups by talking all at once and pointing out the holes in their positions.

SAME and DIFFERENT

What does it mean to be created in God's image? Read the following scriptures, then answer the questions below based on what you discover about God and yourself.

Scriptures: Genesis 1:26-27; 5:1-2; Matthew 5:1-16; and Ephesians 4:13.

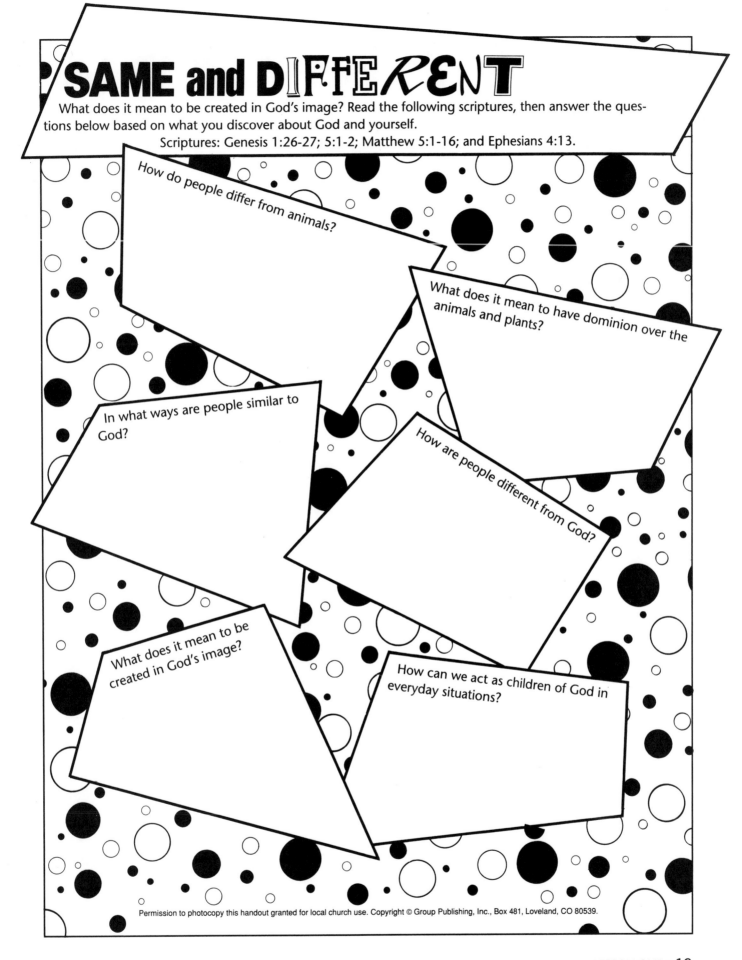

How do people differ from animals?

What does it mean to have dominion over the animals and plants?

In what ways are people similar to God?

How are people different from God?

What does it mean to be created in God's image?

How can we act as children of God in everyday situations?

Table Talk

To the Parent: We're involved in a junior high course at church called *Genesis: The Beginnings*. Students are exploring how learning from the past can help them be better Christians today. We'd like you and your teenager to spend some time discussing this important book of the Bible. Use this "Table Talk" sheet to help you do that.

Parent

Complete the following sentences:
- I think the Bible account of creation is . . .
- When I was a junior higher, I believed the stories in Genesis were . . .
- Being created in God's image means . . .
- One temptation I used to struggle with is . . .
- I felt like God rescued me once when . . .

Junior higher

- I think the Bible account of creation is . . .
- I believe the stories in Genesis are . . .
- Being created in God's image means . . .
- One temptation I struggle with is . . .
- I felt like God rescued me once when . . .

Parent and junior higher

Give your parent/junior higher a gift to represent how you see God's image in him or her. Talk about how you feel as God's child.

Plan a project to celebrate your family history. You might want to make a family tree; assemble a photo album; develop a family slide show; or make a family scrapbook. Work on this project together.

Tell about a time God's protection and grace kept you from danger. Talk about how the story of Noah and the flood is similar to that time.

Read aloud Psalm 8 together. Talk about ways people are less than God and yet still God's most glorious creation. Pray together to more fully understand God's plan for you in his creation.

THE FALL: IT'S SO TEMPTING

Kids face powerful temptations. Whether it's helping a friend cheat on a test or considering taking drugs, the number of temptations teenagers face is alarming. To make things worse, the world often seems to suggest that resisting is too difficult and perhaps even unhealthy.

This misunderstanding can leave young people thinking they're prisoners of temptation. Instead, they need to see they can count on God's grace and strength to resist.

To help junior highers recognize and resist temptation.

Students will:
- **discuss temptation;**
- **explore biblical accounts of people who wrestled with temptation;**
- **develop a specific plan to resist temptation; and**
- **ask God to help them overcome temptation.**

Look up the following scriptures. Then read the background paragraphs to see how the passages relate to your junior highers and middle schoolers.

Genesis 3:1-24 describes Adam and Eve's temptation in the garden.

This passage tells how Adam and Eve traded their innocent relationship with God for the hollow promise of knowing good and evil. Adam and Eve's experience permanently disrupted their relationship with God and brought them spiritual and physical death.

The story of the Fall describes a drastic change in the relationship between humans and God. But it's also a story kids

LESSON AIM

OBJECTIVES

BIBLE BASIS
GENESIS 3:1-24
1 CORINTHIANS 10:13

can relate to in a personal way. Just as Adam and Eve suffered from giving in to temptation, junior highers suffer for giving in to temptation. But kids can be thankful that we have a way back to God through Jesus.

In **1 Corinthians 10:13**, Paul says that no temptation is too great for us to bear.

This passage assures Christians that every temptation is common to the human experience. God has graciously provided a way to escape temptation for those who'll trust him.

Kids often feel that no one else has faced their particular problems. They may also feel trapped by their temptations. Kids can be encouraged to resist temptation, knowing God understands every temptation and always provides a way out.

THIS LESSON AT A GLANCE

Section	Minutes	What Students Will Do	Supplies
Opener (Option 1)	5 to 10	**Pin Me**—Play a game and be tempted to cheat.	Clothespins
(Option 2)		**Twenty Temptations**—Compete to see who can come up with a list of 20 temptations first.	Newsprint, markers, prize
Action and Reflection	10 to 15	**Raid the Cave**—Try to steal a treasure from a guarded "cave."	Masking tape, knotted rag
Bible Application	10 to 15	**What If?**—Discuss Adam and Eve's temptation and talk about how to deal with temptation.	Paper, pencils, Bibles
Commitment	10 to 15	**Prescriptions**—Write prescriptions for resisting temptation.	"Prescriptions" handouts (p. 28), pencils, tape
Closing (Option 1)	up to 5	**Temptation Maze**—Complete a handout and discuss the choices they made.	"Temptation Maze" handouts (p. 29), pencils
(Option 2)		**Toughest Victory**—Write on a card the toughest temptation they've overcome.	3×5 cards, pencils

The Lesson

OPENER
(5 to 10 minutes)

☐ OPTION 1: PIN ME

Give each student five spring-type clothespins. Say: **In the game we're about to play, it's important to follow the rules. On "go," move around the room and clip one clothespin at a time to someone else's clothes. You may** only pin one at a time. When you've pinned all your clothespins, remove clothespins on your clothes one at a time and pin them on someone else.

Don't block someone else from pinning a clothespin on you. You may move out of the way, but using your hands to block someone from pinning you is against the rules. When I call "time," you must stop where you are.

During the game, don't enforce the rules. After four minutes, call time. Have kids count their clothespins. Then have them line up according to the number of clothespins they have—on their clothes and in their hands.

Ask:

● **Did you like this game? Why or why not?** (Yes, it was fun; no, I couldn't clip my clothespins to anyone; no, too many people cheated.)

● **If you weren't doing well, were you tempted to cheat? Explain.** (No, I wanted to follow the rules; yes, other people were cheating so I thought I might.)

● **What were some ways people might've cheated?** (Clipping more than one clothespin at a time; hiding clothespins; blocking people from pinning clothespins.)

● **What might motivate someone to cheat?** (The desire to win; revenge.)

● **What might motivate someone to avoid the temptation to cheat?** (Fear of getting caught; intimidation by other players; desire to follow the rules.)

● **How is this game like other instances when people are tempted?** (You can be tempted and not give in; the temptation to cheat is great in school too.)

Say: **Temptation is something we face daily. Do we cheat on the test or suffer the consequences of not studying? Do we yell at our brother or sister? Do we accept the beer we're offered, even though we know we shouldn't? Today we'll take a look at how a familiar Bible story can help us understand and resist temptations we face.**

☐ OPTION 2: TWENTY TEMPTATIONS

Form teams of no more than four. Give teams each a sheet of newsprint and a marker. Have teams each designate a scribe who'll write on the newsprint. Say: **We all face many temptations every day. On "go," list 20 temptations you might face in a typical week. I'll give you the first one to list, but it'll be up to you to list the rest. The first team to list 20 must call out, "twenty temptations." Then the other teams must stop writing. Write so we can read your ideas. If an idea is illegible or isn't really a temptation, it won't be counted. Also, if you list the same or similar idea twice, it'll only be counted once.**

The team that lists 20 temptations first wins a prize. The first temptation is "cheating on a test." Ready, go!

When a team calls out "twenty temptations," call time. Collect the newsprint sheet from that team and go over the items listed. For questionable items, ask the entire group whether to accept the item. Then count the number of items on each of the other teams' lists and declare the winner. Give a prize (candy or snack food) to the winning team.

Ask:

● **How'd you feel during this game?** (Hurried; frustrated; anxious.)

● **Were you tempted to cheat? Explain.** (No, I couldn't think of any way to cheat; yes, I was going to steal ideas from other teams.)

● **How is being tempted to cheat in this game like the temptations you just listed?** (Sometimes you need help to win, so you're tempted to cheat; when you're going after a prize it's easy to be tempted to do whatever needs to be done to get the prize.)

Have kids vote on which temptation listed is most common and which is most rare.

Say: **Some of the temptations we face are small. And some are major potentially life-changing temptations. But whatever the size, we all face temptations. Today we'll take a look at a familiar Bible story that can help us better understand temptation and how to resist it.**

Table Talk Follow-Up

If you sent the "Table Talk" handout (p. 20) to parents last week, discuss students' reactions to the activity. Ask volunteers to share what they learned from the discussion with their parents.

ACTION AND REFLECTION
(10 to 15 minutes)

RAID THE CAVE

You'll need a large room for this activity—or you may do it outside. Use masking tape to mark off a 10×10-foot area. This will be the "bear's cave."

Place a knotted rag—the treasure—in the center of the cave. Have a volunteer be the "bear" who'll guard the treasure. The rest of the students must try to swipe the treasure without being tagged by the bear. The bear may not pick up the treasure. People tagged inside the cave must freeze where they are. The person who gets the treasure becomes the next bear. If no one gets the treasure within two minutes, the bear wins and a new bear is picked.

Explain the game to the students. Then play for eight minutes. Kids will probably become frustrated if they can't get the treasure or if they can't guard it well. That's okay; you'll discuss their feelings after the game.

When time is up, regroup for a discussion.

Ask:

● **How'd you feel as you played this game? Explain.**

(Anxious, I didn't want to get caught; confident, I knew I could win.)

● **What risks did you take in this game?** (Running into the cave; trying to dodge being tagged.)

● **How are those risks like the risks we take when we give in to temptation?** (We might suffer the consequences; we could get in trouble; we usually won't be able to avoid getting caught.)

● **Did you choose to race right in or wait outside the cave for the right opportunity? Explain.** (I ran right in because I wanted to be first; I waited to see what others would do.)

● **Did you enjoy the risks in this game? Explain.** (Yes, I liked taking risks; no, I didn't want to be caught.)

● **How is the way you played this game like the way you face risk in everyday situations?** (I'm cautious about the risks; I'm not afraid to take a risk once in a while.)

Say: **Sometimes, the risks associated with temptation seem minor. But when we give in to temptation, we're risking more than being tagged in a game.**

Ask:

● **What are risks associated with temptations you face in real life?** (Getting caught cheating; getting drunk; hurting a friend's feelings.)

Say: **To better understand temptation, let's take a look at the familiar story of Adam and Eve.**

WHAT IF?

Form groups of no more than five. Give groups each paper, pencils and a Bible.

Say: **Read aloud Genesis 3. Then talk about what might've happened if Adam and Eve hadn't given in to temptation.** Allow three minutes for groups to read and discuss the chapter in Genesis.

Then ask:

● **What made it difficult for Adam and Eve to resist the temptation to eat the fruit?** (They were tricked; they wanted to gain knowledge.)

● **How is this situation like the temptations you face?** (We don't always know the consequences; we're sometimes tricked by friends.)

Tell kids about a time when you gave in to temptation. Then have volunteers each tell about a time when they gave in to temptation.

Ask:

● **How might things have been different if you hadn't given in to temptation?** (I wouldn't have gotten in trouble; I would've stayed sober; I would've done better on the test.)

Have kids read aloud Hebrews 2:18; 4:15; and 1 Corinthians 10:13.

BIBLE APPLICATION
(10 to 15 minutes)

Ask:

● **How can these verses help us overcome temptations we face?** (They remind us nothing is too great a temptation; they remind us Jesus was able to overcome temptation.)

Form new groups of no more than three. Have groups each quickly come up with a tempting situation they might face. Then, one by one, have groups act out their situation up to the point where someone must decide whether to give in to the temptation. For example, a group might role play kids asking friends to go with them to a questionable movie.

When the skit is stopped, have other kids call out ways to avoid the temptation. For example, kids might say, "Say no and walk away" or "Tell your friends they shouldn't go."

After groups have presented their skits, reread 1 Corinthians 10:13 aloud. Say: **We learn from Genesis 3 that giving in to temptation can have disastrous results. But we learn from the New Testament that no temptation is too great to overcome. Still, it's not always easy to know the right thing to do in tempting situations. Let's take a few minutes to create a plan for dealing with temptations.**

COMMITMENT
(10 to 15 minutes)

PRESCRIPTIONS

Distribute a "Prescriptions" handout (p. 28) and a pencil to each person. Form pairs.

Say: **Jesus was tempted in every way that you and I are. Yet he didn't sin. He understands how difficult it is to resist temptation. He wants to encourage us to be strong and not give in to temptation.**

In fact, God has made a way for us to escape every temptation that comes our way. With your partner, write a prescription for the best way to resist temptation. In your prescription, include practical ways to overcome temptation such as "avoid tempting situations" and "ask God to help you." Imagine that Jesus is writing this prescription to you and your friends. In a few minutes we'll read some of these prescriptions.

Allow four to six minutes for partners to complete their prescriptions. Be available during this time to help kids.

Then have kids each read their prescription to the class. After each prescription is read, have kids say what they liked about it. For example, someone might say, "Your prescription is practical" or "Your prescription is well-thought-out." Encourage kids to share only positive thoughts for each prescription read.

Tape the handouts to the wall. Say: **Think about a temptation you're facing. Then silently come up to this wall and read the prescriptions. Choose one or more idea from these prescriptions to use in the coming week as you face temptation.**

Keep the prescriptions on the wall for a few weeks to remind kids they can resist temptation.

☐ OPTION 1: TEMPTATION MAZE

Give kids each a "Temptation Maze" handout (p. 29) and a pencil. Have kids each complete the maze according to the instructions on their handout. Then form groups of no more than three. Have kids compare their completed handouts and discuss how they handle temptation.

Form a circle. Say: **Sometimes temptations look like the maze you just completed. You may see the options but not know which way to turn. With support from each other and God's guidance, we can know which way to turn.**

Close with prayer, asking God to help you avoid tempting situations.

☐ OPTION 2: TOUGHEST VICTORY

Form groups of no more than five. Give kids each a 3×5 card and a pencil.

Say: **On your 3×5 card, write one of the toughest temptations you've been able to resist or overcome by God's grace. Don't put your name on the card. After you finish, tear your card into as many pieces as there are people in your group. Give one scrap to each person in your circle.**

Carry these scraps in your wallet or purse this week to remind you to pray for the people in your group. Ask God to make each of you strong enough to overcome whatever temptations come this week. The scraps will also remind you that others are praying for you.

Form a large circle. Have kids each offer a one-sentence prayer asking God to help them resist temptation in the coming week.

C L O S I N G
(up to 5 minutes)

If You Still Have Time . . .

Domino Effect—Have kids discuss how giving in to temptations can affect other people. For example, have kids talk about how one person's decision to take drugs might affect his or her friends and family.

Dear Expert—Have three or four kids form a panel at the front of the room. Ask kids each to write one tempting situation on a 3×5 card. These could include the temptation to gossip, take drugs, get drunk, or cheat on a test.

Give the cards to the panel and have panel members describe specific ways to avoid the temptations.

R_X PRESCRIPTIONS

Jesus was tempted in every way—just as we are—yet he didn't sin. Because Jesus was tempted, he's able to help those who are tempted. God is faithful; he won't let you be tempted beyond what you can handle. But when you're tempted, he'll provide a way out so you can stand up to the temptation. Adapted from Hebrews 2:18; 4:15; and 1 Corinthians 10:13.

Imagine you're a spiritual doctor with a specialization in resisting temptation. In consultation with your partner, write a prescription for resisting temptation to be used by junior highers.

To resist temptation . . .

TEMPTATION MAZE

Draw a single line that doesn't cross itself from "Start" (upper-left corner) to "Finish" (lower-right corner). When your line crosses an apple, read the temptation associated with that letter and continue drawing your line in the direction indicated by your answer. When you reach the end, total the number of stars and circles your line crossed through. List these in the space provided. Then refer to the scoring table below and compare your scores to other group members' scores.

Temptations

A You find $5 on the floor next to a teacher's desk.
Go east if you keep it and don't tell anyone you found it.
Go west if you tell the teacher about the money.
Go south if you leave the money on the floor.

B Your friend promises to treat you to ice cream if you tell his parents he stayed overnight at your house last night. You know he really went to a party with friends.
Go south if you tell him you'll do it.
Go east if you tell him "no way."

C Your friends are skipping gym. They ask you to join them.
Go east if you do it.
Go south if you tell your friends it's wrong to skip class.
Go north if you make up a story so your friends won't think you're scared to skip class.

D Your friend offers you a pass to a popular R-rated film. She knows how to get in the movie without an adult.
Go west if you accept the pass and go to the movie.
Go east if you "pass" on the pass.

E You need to finish an English paper by tomorrow. A friend who gets good grades tells you she'll write the paper for $10.
Go east if you pay your friend to write the paper.
Go north if you stay up late to finish the paper yourself.

F You find that the candy machine in the cafeteria is broken. You can get as many candy bars as you want for free.
Go north if you take a bunch of candy bars before telling a teacher about the machine.
Go south if you don't take any free candy bars and tell a teacher about the broken machine.

G Your friends offer you a beer between classes.
Go east if you drink the beer so friends don't laugh at you.
Go south if you simply say "no" and leave.
Go west if you report the students' illegal activities to a school counselor.

H A girl or guy you really like asks you to play a mean trick on one of your friends.
Go west if you agree to help plan the mean trick.
Go east if you tell this person you won't help him or her.

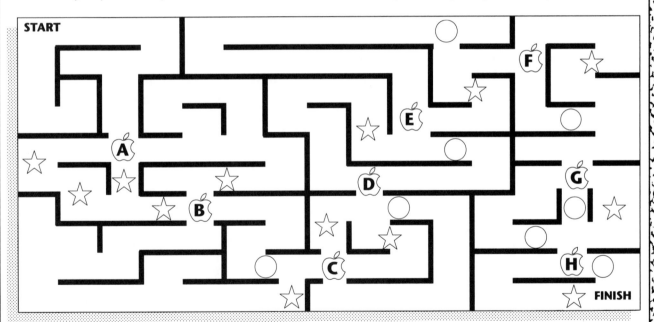

Scoring:
1 point for each star: ☆ _____
3 points for each circle: ○ _____
Total your points: _____

How'd you do?
20 to 24 points—Congrats! You know how to resist temptation. Keep up the good work. (Or did you cheat by looking at this first? If you did, read the comments for 8 to 13 below.)

14 to 19—You know how to avoid temptations, but you still give in once in a while. Talk with someone about ways to improve your temptation-resistance.

8 to 13—Danger! Your temptation-resistance is near zero. Find a trusted friend and tell him or her about your inability to resist temptation. Consider talking with a pastor or youth worker. And don't forget, God provides a way out of temptation.

LESSON 3

GIVING YOUR BEST

Many people and activities vie for top priority in junior highers' lives. It's often too easy for kids to put their relationship with God aside, because it doesn't seem as urgent as other things. Kids need to see the importance of making their relationship with God top priority in their lives.

LESSON AIM

To help junior highers learn what it means to give their best to God.

OBJECTIVES

Students will:
- experience giving their best effort in an activity;
- explore what the story of Cain and Abel says about giving God your best;
- discover what it means to give their best to God; and
- commit to make their relationship with God top priority in their lives.

BIBLE BASIS

GENESIS 4:1-15
MATTHEW 6:33

Look up the following scriptures. Then read the background paragraphs to see how the passages relate to your junior highers and middle schoolers.

In **Genesis 4:1-15**, Cain kills his brother, Abel.

This familiar story describes how important it is to give God your best. The story also tells how God promised Cain a restored relationship if he went out and did well.

Junior highers probably understand what it means to do well at school. But they may not understand what it means to do well as a Christian. This passage can help kids understand that God wants them to give him their best efforts.

In **Matthew 6:33**, Jesus tells the multitudes to seek the

kingdom of God above all else.

This verse comes in the context of how to deal with anxiety. When Jesus tells us to seek God first, he's telling us to trust God to take care of us. But there's another message in this verse—God needs to be the center of our lives.

When it comes to seeking advice, junior highers often look to parents and peers. But this passage suggests the need to go to God first with our concerns, joys and problems.

THIS LESSON AT A GLANCE

Section	Minutes	What Students Will Do	Supplies
Opener (Option 1)	5 to 10	**Best Effort**—Use varying amounts of effort to play a game.	Ping-Pong balls, paper cups
(Option 2)		**What's Best?**—Make lists of things that are "bests."	Tape, newsprint, markers
Action and Reflection	10 to 15	**Second Best?**—Create sculptures and get prizes for their sculptures.	Plastic straws, marsh-mallows, prizes
Bible Application	10 to 15	**Right Attitude**—Discover what the Bible says about giving their best to God.	Bibles, cookies
Commitment	10 to 15	**Giving Your Best**—Commit to give their best to God in specific ways.	"What I'll Give" hand-outs (p. 36), pencils, cookies
Closing (Option 1)	up to 5	**Top Priority**—Write a note to God, telling him they want to make their relationship with him top priority.	Paper, pencils, envelope, tape
(Option 2)		**Best Prayer**—Develop a prayer together asking God to help them give their best to him.	Tape, newsprint, marker

The Lesson

☐ OPTION 1: BEST EFFORT

Form pairs. Give pairs each a Ping-Pong ball and a paper cup. Have partners stand 4 feet apart, facing each other. Have one partner (the catcher) hold the cup and the other (the tosser) hold the Ping-Pong ball. Say: **The object of this game is to get the ball in the cup. But along the way, I'll give you instructions to tell you how to do that. Begin by taking a practice toss or two. You may move the cup to try to catch the ball, but you may not move your feet.**

OPENER
(5 to 10 minutes)

Have kids toss the Ping-Pong ball into the cup a few times. Then say: **Move back three big steps and try again.** After a few more tries, say: **Catchers, stop trying to catch the ball.** After a few more tries, say: **Tossers, give only a marginal effort to get the ball in the cup.** After a few more tries, say: **Now move back three more large steps. Tosser and catcher, give your best effort to get the ball in the cup.** After a few more tries, call time.

Ask:

● **How'd it feel to toss the ball into the cup the first time?** (Great; okay; no big deal.)

● **How important was your effort in this activity? Explain.** (Very important, it was tough to get the ball in the cup; somewhat important, it was real easy.)

● **How'd your effort change between the first stage and the last stage of the game?** (We had to work harder in the end; it was the same.)

● **If you got the ball in during the last stage of the activity, how'd you feel?** (Great; I knew we could do it; it was fun.)

● **How important is putting our best effort into things?** (Very important; it depends on the activity.)

Say: **Today we're going to look at the effort we put into our relationship with God. God wants our best, but do we give it to him? Let's find out.**

☐ OPTION 2: WHAT'S BEST?

Tape five sheets of newsprint to the wall. On each, write one of the following headings: food, movie, free-time activity, school subject, and music group or artist.

Give kids each a marker, and have them write on each newsprint sheet one or more items they think are best in that category. For example, kids might write "ice cream, steak, or vegetables" for the food list.

Have kids each explain which item in each list they'd consider best, and why. For each category, have kids vote on the best item in the list. Circle the winning item for each list.

Ask:

● **How easy was it to choose the best item in each category? Explain.** (Easy, I picked what I liked; tough, there were so many good things.)

● **What characteristics help make these things the best?** (Quality of the item; attention to detail; color; taste.)

● **What goes into making something "the best"?** (Care; lots of time; hard work.)

● **What kinds of activities do you put your best into?** (Sports; school; relationships.)

Say: **Each of us may have a different opinion on what is the best food or the best movie. And we may put our best efforts into different activities. But God wants our best too. Today we'll learn how to give God our best.**

SECOND BEST?

Form groups of no more than five. Give groups each plastic straws and marshmallows. Say: **We're going to have a contest to see who can create the most beautiful sculpture out of the marshmallows and straws. These sculptures should represent God's love for us. The winning sculpture will get a special prize.**

Encourage kids to be creative. Allow six minutes for groups to complete their sculptures. Then have groups each explain their sculpture to the rest of the class.

Walk up to one sculpture and say: **This sculpture represents a great amount of effort. And a prize goes to this team for its hard work.**

Give the team a prize. Then walk up to another sculpture and say the same thing. Give that team a prize too. Do this for all the sculptures.

Then ask:

● **How'd you feel when the first sculpture was awarded a prize?** (I felt bad that ours didn't win; I was happy for the group that made it.)

● **How'd you feel when I began to award a prize for all of the sculptures?** (Happy; confused; surprised.)

● **How is giving your best different from being the best?** (Giving your best doesn't always mean you'll be the best; giving your best is effort, being the best is a result of effort.)

● **How is giving your best effort in this activity like giving your best to God?** (You give your best to God because of the prize you receive; it's easy to give your best to God; sometimes it's tough to get motivated to give your best.)

● **How is the result of this activity like the result of our giving our best to God?** (We all get rewarded; we all benefit from our efforts; God is pleased with all our efforts.)

Say: **God desires our best. But sometimes we don't feel like giving our best to him—or we don't have the right attitude. Let's take a close look at the story of Cain and Abel to see just what God wants from us.**

RIGHT ATTITUDE

Have someone read aloud Genesis 4:1-15. Then form groups of no more than five. Have groups each briefly discuss the following questions:

● **Why didn't God accept Cain's offering?**

● **Why was Cain upset at God?**

● **Based on this passage, how important is it to give God your best effort?**

Form a circle. Have kids each say how they'd feel if they were in Cain's situation.

Ask:

● **Have you ever felt like Cain did after his offering wasn't accepted? Explain.** (Yes, sometimes I feel like God expects too much; no, I know God expects a lot, but he gives me more than one chance to give my best.)

Give kids each a cookie, but tell them not to eat it. Say: **It may seem unfair, but God doesn't want our second-best effort. Just as Abel gave the best sacrifice he had to God, we must give the best we have to offer. Imagine that your cookie represents the "best" you give to God.**

Think about what it means for you to give your best to God. For example, you might think giving your best to God means going to church regularly. In a minute, each of you will come to the front of the room and tell what giving your best to God means to you, then place your cookie on this "altar" (point to a nearby table).

Allow kids one minute to think about what it means to give their best to God. Then have kids each take a turn saying what giving their best to God means and place their cookie on the altar. Be sure to include yourself in this activity. When kids each have placed their cookie on the altar, collect the cookies and hide them or take them to another class.

Form a circle and ask:
● **Was it easy to describe what it means to give your best to God? Why or why not?** (No, I didn't know what to say; yes, I could think of a lot of things to say.)
● **How'd you feel when I took your cookies away?** (Angry; upset; confused.)

Say: **Sometimes giving our best to God will require sacrifice. Just as you gave your cookie away, you may have to give up something you like in order to give God your best efforts. For example, if you enjoy spending time with friends, but friends are interfering with your relationship with God, you may have to limit your time with friends.**

Have kids call out other ways they might have to sacrifice to give their best to God. Read aloud Matthew 6:33. Ask:
● **What does it mean to seek God first?** (Ask God before doing anything; trust God to help you.)

Say: **In this passage, Jesus speaks about trusting God to take care of us. But the key words in the passage, "seek first," tell us something else about God. He wants our relationship with him to be the focus of our lives. By seeking God first, we'll learn to give him our best.**

COMMITMENT
(10 to 15 minutes)

GIVING YOUR BEST

Give kids each a "What I'll Give" handout (p. 36) and a pencil. Have kids complete the handout.

Form groups of no more than four. Have kids discuss their handouts with their group members. Ask kids each to share at least one thing they plan to do to give their best to God.

Then form a circle. Say: **Earlier, we discovered how sometimes giving God our best may require sacrifice. But when we give God our best, we often see rewards come back.**

Go around the circle, and give kids each a new cookie. If

possible, make these cookies nicer than the ones you hid or gave away earlier. Tell kids the cookies represent God's response to their willingness to give him their best. As you give kids each a cookie, tell them one thing you appreciate about their relationship with God. For example, you might say, "I appreciate your willingness to learn more about God" or "I'm glad you're committed to serving God first."

After you've gone around the circle, allow kids to walk around and congratulate each other for their commitments.

☐ OPTION 1: TOP PRIORITY

Give kids each a sheet of paper and a pencil. Say: **In order to give our best to God, we each need to make our relationship with him top priority in life. On your paper, write a brief note to God, telling him you want to make your relationship with him your top priority. If you don't feel comfortable telling this to God, use your note to ask God how you can make him top priority.**

Allow two minutes for kids to write their notes. Then collect the notes and place them in an envelope. Tape the envelope to the ceiling or high on a wall in the room. Say: **Just as I've placed this envelope high in the room, let us make our relationship with God a high priority in our lives.**

Close with a moment of silent prayer. Leave the envelope taped to the ceiling to remind kids to give their best to God.

☐ OPTION 2: BEST PRAYER

Tape a sheet of newsprint to the wall. Say: **Together, we're going to write a prayer to God, asking him to help us give our best to him. One at a time, silently come up to the newsprint and write a portion of the prayer. You don't need to say much, but be honest and focus on how we can give God our best.**

Start things off by using a marker to write the opening to the prayer. Then encourage kids each to add a few words or a sentence to the prayer. When the prayer is complete, have kids gather around it and read it in unison as your closing.

CLOSING
(up to 5 minutes)

If You Still Have Time . . .

Best Ideas—Have kids brainstorm how they can challenge their friends to give their best to God. Encourage kids to think of creative ways to share the importance of a relationship with God. Talk about how easy or difficult it is to tell someone about the importance of a relationship with God.

Best Pantomimes—Form groups of no more than five. Have groups each pantomime an action that shows kids giving God their best in situations at school, home or church. For example, kids might pantomime helping others at school or studying the Bible. Afterward, have kids talk about ways they can give God their best in their relationships with others.

WHAT I'LL GIVE

What does it mean to give God your best? It might mean spending more time in prayer. Or it might mean trusting God to help you overcome temptations. Think about your relationship with God. Then draw a picture to represent your relationship in the box. What does your picture say about the priority you give your relationship with God?

Complete the following sentences with specific ways you'll give your best to God. For example, for the "school" sentence you might write, "I'll be more open about my relationship with God when I talk with friends."

One way I'll give my best to God while at home is . . .

One way I'll give my best to God while at school is . . .

One way I'll give my best to God at church is . . .

One way I'll give my best to God every day is . . .

THE FLOOD: GOD TO THE RESCUE

Young teenagers often feel like helpless captives of their circumstances. They can be paralyzed by their inability to be and do all they wish for themselves. By helping kids understand the redemption Jesus Christ offers all who trust him, we can free them from this powerlessness.

To help junior highers trust God to rescue them from difficult situations.

LESSON AIM

Students will:
- **experience what it's like to be rescued;**
- **discover evidences of Noah's faith;**
- **learn why it's important to trust God; and**
- **thank God for rescuing them.**

OBJECTIVES

Look up the following scriptures. Then read the background paragraphs to see how the passages relate to your junior highers and middle schoolers.

In **Genesis 6:1—9:29**, God calls Noah to build an ark.

By Noah's time, evil had gotten out of control. Yet Noah and God had a good relationship. When Noah emerged from the ark after the flood, he gave God an offering of thanks, and God promised never to destroy the world again by flood. God made a solemn covenant with the people he saved.

With environmental problems, terrorism and natural disasters all around, junior highers may see today's world as being out of control. By trusting Christ, they can experience God's rescue for themselves. Junior highers may think of God as distant and casually receive his good gifts. But when they recognize how wonderful a relationship with God is, they can live with thankful confidence.

BIBLE BASIS
GENESIS 6:1—9:29
HEBREWS 11:7

The author of **Hebrews 11:7** describes how Noah had to trust God.

Noah had to trust that God was giving the right instructions to build the ark. By exercising that faith, he was rescued by God and inherited God's righteousness.

Junior highers who are struggling to be good enough for their friends and parents can be free of this pressure by trusting Jesus Christ to give them his righteousness.

THIS LESSON AT A GLANCE

Section	Minutes	What Students Will Do	Supplies
Opener (Option 1)	up to 5	**Faith Fall**—Experience how it feels to trust someone.	
(Option 2)		**Trust Search**—Find an object that reminds them of a time they trusted someone.	
Action and Reflection	15 to 20	**The Best Way Out**—Determine how they'd respond to practical dilemmas.	Tape, "Good" and "Lousy" signs
Bible Application	10 to 15	**Faith Charades**—Pantomime evidences of Noah's faith.	Bibles
Commitment	10 to 15	**Faith Sculptures**—Sculpt models of their relationship with God.	Pipe cleaners, Bible
Closing (Option 1)	up to 5	**Thanks, God**—Write notes to God, thanking him for rescuing them from sin.	Paper, pencils
(Option 2)		**How's Your TQ?**—Evaluate their "thanks quotient."	"How's Your TQ?" handouts (p. 43), pencils

The Lesson

OPENER
(up to 5 minutes)

☐ OPTION 1: FAITH FALL

Form groups of five to eight people. If you have a group smaller than five, have kids in this group join other groups. Have kids stand shoulder to shoulder in their circles with one person standing alone in the middle of the circle. Have kids in the circle put their arms in front of them to catch the person in the middle. Tell kids in the center each to cross their arms over their chest, keep their feet still and knees locked. Have kids in the center each keep their eyes closed and fall stiffly toward the people in the circle. Tell kids in the circle to gently pass the person in the middle around the circle. Have kids take turns being in the center of the circle.

After three or four minutes, ask:

● **How'd you feel as you were passed around the circle?** (Uncomfortable; nervous; confident.)

● **How is this like the feeling you have when you have to trust others to help you in everyday life?** (I feel confident when a friend promises to help; I feel nervous when I have to trust someone to do something for me.)

Say: **Trust is a difficult thing to develop. But sometimes we have to rely on others to help us make it through. Today we'll take a look at how our trust in God can rescue us from difficult times.**

☐ OPTION 2: TRUST SEARCH

Form groups of no more than six. Say: **Search this room for objects that remind you of specific occasions when you overcame a limitation by trusting a person or God. For example, you might pick up a Bible and tell about a time you read a passage that helped you trust God more. The person whose first name's first initial is first in the alphabet will begin.**

After the first person finds an object and tells about it, have the next person in alphabetical order go on a similar search. Encourage kids each to describe their object and tell their story quickly.

After everyone has found and described an object, call the kids together and form a circle.

Ask:

● **How'd you feel as you described your trust experience?** (I was uncomfortable; I didn't like it; I felt good.)

● **What'd you learn from the stories your group members told?** (We all have to trust others; sometimes it's difficult to trust others.)

Say: **Today we're going to explore what it means to trust God. We'll begin by examining ways our faith can help us escape dilemmas.**

THE BEST WAY OUT

Tape a "Good" sign to a wall at one end of the room and a "Lousy" at the other. Clear the furniture from the center of the room so students can move easily between the signs. Have kids stand facing you in the middle of the room.

Say: **Today we're exploring how God rescues people who trust him. To get a feeling for the escape routes we choose, I'm going to read possible ways out of situations you might face. If you agree that the escape plan described is a good one, walk to the end of the room with the "Good" sign. If you think it isn't a good plan, walk to the "Lousy" sign. If you aren't sure how you feel, stand somewhere in the middle.**

Read the "Escape Plans" (p. 40) one at a time. Allow time

ACTION AND REFLECTION
(15 to 20 minutes)

for kids to find their positions between the "Good" and "Lousy" signs. After kids move, ask:

- **Why do you think this is or isn't a good way to get out of this problem?**
- **What alternate plans could you suggest?**
- **How do you think God might help someone out of a fix like this?**

Before you finish reading the last situation, stop the activity suddenly and say: **Something's wrong here. Hear that sound?** (pause) **It seems our room is filling up with water. The doors are blocked and the windows locked shut. You have two minutes to decide how you'll respond to this situation. I'll keep you posted on how high the water is. Right now it's up to your ankles.**

Have kids band together to discuss how they'll try to escape the flood. If they come up with a plan they think will work, quickly give them a reason it won't work. For example, if kids say they can climb through the ceiling tiles to escape, tell them the tiles are blocked on the other side. Every 15 seconds, update kids with the height of the water. After a minute, the water should be up to the shortest member's neck. Have kids work together to stay above the water as they talk about what they'll do. Be sure to play along and keep your head above the water line too.

After two minutes (or when the water level is about to cover someone's head), gather kids in a circle and pray, asking God to rescue them from this flood. Then say: **Wait . . . the water's stopped coming in. In fact it's subsiding.**

Let kids know when the water is finally out of the room. Then form a circle. Hand out imaginary towels and ask:

- **How'd you feel when the "flood" started to enter the room?** (I thought it was silly; I thought you were serious; it was weird.)
- **How'd you feel when our prayer "rescued" us from the water?** (Relieved; happy; I was surprised.)
- **How is this situation like times when God helps you through a difficult situation?** (I feel relieved when I get out of a tough situation; I'm usually surprised when God rescues me.)
- **What are some ways God rescues you from difficult situations?** (He builds my confidence to stand up for what I believe; he brings me comfort when I feel uncomfortable.)

Escape Plans

1. Your friends ask you to go to the mall the same day your mother wants you to help with a birthday party for your little sister. When they pressure you to come along, you tell them you have too much homework.

2. The lunch room is noisier than usual. Every time the lunch-room monitor turns her back, a french fry flies. You know a food fight is about to start so you say to your friends, "I think I'll go to the library to study for next week's math test."

3. While playing a pick-up baseball game in the street, you hit a home run off your neighbor's car and put a dent in the hood. After you tag home, you keep running back to your house.

4. A fight breaks out in the aisle next to your table in the lunch room at school. You jump between the two who are fighting to get them to stop slugging each other.

5. You're at a friend's house with several kids, studying for next week's history test. Your friend's parents aren't home. Your friend offers everyone a beer. You take the beer and pour it into a house plant a little at a time so no one will notice you're not drinking it.

6. Your friends are planning to go to a popular but violent horror movie, and they invite you to join them. You really don't enjoy getting scared and don't want to see the movie. You say, "I heard that film was terrible. I don't want to see it."

Say: **Our flood was nothing compared to the flood Noah endured. Let's see what we can learn from how Noah responded to his situation.**

FAITH CHARADES

Form groups of no more than three. Have groups each find a place in the room away from other groups. Give each group a Bible.

Have groups each read aloud Hebrews 11:7, paying attention to what it says about Noah's faith. Then have groups search for evidence of Noah's faith in the account of the flood in Genesis 6:1—9:29.

Have groups each choose one evidence of Noah's faith to act out in a charade for the entire class to guess. Tell kids each charade is to be acted out without props or speaking.

Allow groups five minutes to find something to act out. Then have groups each perform their charade. After each charade, have group members guess what the charade portrayed. Then have the group members who performed the charade tell what they were presenting about Noah's faith.

Ask:

● **What'd you discover about Noah's faith?** (He had a great trust in God; he listened to God even when his friends laughed at him.)

● **What can we learn about faith from this story?** (We need to trust God even when it's tough; God follows through on his promises.)

Say: **Trust is an important element of our relationship with others. Without trust, we can't develop a healthy relationship with people. It's the same way with God. We may not always get the response we want, but if we trust God he'll help us find an "escape plan" for difficult situations.**

FAITH SCULPTURES

Form a circle. Give each kid a pipe cleaner.

Have a volunteer read aloud Genesis 9:12-16. Then say: **Think for a couple of minutes about your faith in God. How has Christ rescued you? In what ways could you picture your relationship with Jesus? Shape your pipe cleaner into a sculpture that illustrates your relationship with God.**

Allow two or three minutes for kids to create their sculptures. Then have kids each describe their sculpture.

Ask:

● **How do you feel about your relationship with God?** (Comfortable; I need to work on it; I don't know.)

● **Why is it important to trust God?** (Trusting God helps us know what to do; trusting God gets us out of tough situations.)

BIBLE APPLICATION
(10 to 15 minutes)

COMMITMENT
(10 to 15 minutes)

Ask kids to silently make a commitment to trust God more. If you have any non-Christians in your class, this could be a good opportunity to present the gospel message to them.

Thank kids for sharing. Then string your sculptured pipe cleaner on another pipe cleaner. As you do, say one thing you like about the meaning of the sculpture created by the person on your left. For example, you might say, "I'm glad your relationship with Jesus is strong" or "I appreciate your honesty about your relationship with Jesus." Have kids each string their sculpture onto the pipe cleaner as they say something positive about the person's sculpture on their left.

☐ OPTION 1: THANKS, GOD

Give kids each a sheet of paper and a pencil. Have kids each write a thank-you note to God, expressing thanks for being rescued from sin. Encourage them to write how good it feels to be forgiven and to be strong enough, through faith, to overcome life's problems. Then have kids draw a picture on the paper representing thankfulness. Have kids each describe their picture to someone else in the class.

Have kids each take their note home as a reminder of their faith and God's grace. Have volunteers close in prayer, thanking God for rescuing them.

☐ OPTION 2: HOW'S YOUR TQ?

Give kids each a "How's Your TQ?" handout (p. 43) and a pencil. Have kids each complete their handout. Say: **These handouts won't be shared with anyone else, so don't be shy filling them out. When you've completed the handout, take a couple of minutes to reflect on your score. Then think of ways you can be more thankful each day.**

Form a circle, and close by having kids thank God for rescuing them from difficult situations. Encourage kids to keep their handouts as reminders to be thankful for all God's done for them.

CLOSING
(up to 5 minutes)

If You Still Have Time . . .

Faith Definitions—Form groups of no more than three. Have groups each write a definition of faith in God. Have groups each read their definition to the rest of the class. Then have kids discuss how difficult it is to describe faith to people who don't know Jesus. Have kids brainstorm practical ways to tell their non-Christian friends about trusting God.

Course Reflection—Form a circle. Ask students to reflect on the past four lessons. Have them take turns completing the following sentences:
● Something I learned in this course was . . .
● If I could tell my friends about this course, I'd say . . .
● Something I'll do differently because of this course is . . .

HOW'S YOUR TQ?

Fill in the blanks and write your score in the column on the right.

1. Write the name of one friend you said "thank you" to this past week. _____
Give yourself 5 points for writing the name and 10 more points if you remember
what you said "thank you" for.   POINTS_____

2. Write the name of one family member you said thank you to this past week. _____
Give yourself 5 points for writing the name and 10 more points if you
remember what you said "thank you" for.   POINTS_____

3. Give yourself 15 points if you wrote a thank-you note to someone
this week.   POINTS_____

4. Think back to your last birthday or Christmas (whichever is freshest in your memory)
and list your gifts.

_____

_____

_____

Give yourself 1 point for each gift you can remember saying "thank you" for and
5 extra points for each one you wrote a thank-you note for.   POINTS_____

5. In 30 seconds, list gifts God has given you.

_____

_____

_____

Give yourself 1 point for each gift you can list and 5 extra points if you already
thanked God today.   POINTS_____

6. When was the last time you thanked Jesus for dying to rescue you from sin?

_____

_____

Give yourself 1 point if it's been more than a year, 5 points if it's been less than a
year but more than a month, 10 points for less than a month but more than a week,
15 points for less than a week, and 20 points if you did it today. You can still get
20 points by thanking him now, before you write the number.   POINTS_____
Now total your points and put your total "TQ" here.   TOTAL_____

Less than 30 points   Think of ways you can be more thankful.
31 to 74 points   Keep on thanking!
Over 75 points   Spread the contagious thank you!

BONUS IDEAS

The Nature of Things—Plan a field trip that emphasizes the study of nature. Consider going to a local, state or national park; a natural history museum; a nature center; or a biology or zoology department of a local college.

If possible, have kids participate in a worship service at the site as recognition of the wonder of God's creation.

Afterward, have kids share what they felt during the trip. Use Psalm 148 as a starting place for talking about how God is honored by his creation.

Genesis Skits—Have kids write and perform skits based on the stories in Genesis covered by this course. Encourage kids to be creative in their adaptation of the stories. Then have kids perform these skits for the whole church or children's classes.

TV Test Pattern—Give kids each a "Test Pattern" handout (p. 47), and have them complete it during the week. Then meet to discuss how television portrays God's world and his people. Talk about how commercials and programs often make us seem like less than God's best. Close the meeting by sharing ways we see God in each other.

Doc Talk—Invite a Christian psychologist or psychiatrist to talk with your group about the importance of self-esteem. Have your guest discuss how knowing we're made in God's image can help us have a good self-image. Include activities to boost self-esteem, such as: working together to build something; having kids say what they appreciate about each other; and having kids give each other gifts that symbolize something they admire in each other.

Wonders of the World—Have kids collect pictures depicting the wonder of God's creation, and include them on a wall mural in your church. Have kids add drawings, sayings and Bible passages to the mural. Consider having the entire congregation sign a section of the mural where kids have written: "I'm created in God's image. Lord, help me live like I deserve that honor."

Leave the mural up for a month to remind church members how important they are to God.

More Genesis Stories—Use meetings from *Fun Old Testament Bible Studies* (Group Books) to delve deeper into the

MEETINGS AND MORE

book of Genesis. *Fun Old Testament Bible Studies* includes five lessons from Genesis covering such topics as: building faith; receiving forgiveness; and facing sin's alienation.

Table Talk—Use the "Table Talk" handout (p. 20) as the basis for a meeting with parents and teenagers. During the meeting, have parents and kids complete the handout and discuss it. Include fun activities for parents and kids to do together. Check out *Quick Crowdbreakers and Games for Youth Groups* (Group Books) for fun game ideas.

PARTY PLEASER

Photo Party—Invite kids and their parents to bring family pictures, videos and movies to a party celebrating family histories. You might want to limit the number of pictures, videos and movies each family can bring. Have families each take a turn presenting their "photo history" to the whole group. Ask parents and kids each to tell one thing they appreciate about their history.

During the meeting, serve lots of fun family foods such as pizza, popcorn and ice cream. Discuss how Genesis is a "family history" of God's people. Read Genesis 1:26-27, and discuss how it feels to be created in God's image. Discuss how the stories of God's family in Genesis are similar to families' stories today.

RETREAT IDEA

God's Great Creation Retreat—Arrange to have an overnight camping retreat at a unique site in your area, such as: a cave, a waterfall, a mountain, a forest, a desert or some other wonder of nature. Include a study of Psalm 19 in a program that focuses on the wonder of creation. During the overnight retreat, have kids each express appreciation for God's creation in a creative way, such as: a skit, a song or a poem. Remember to practice and teach sound environmental habits while you're camping. For example, pack your trash, and don't hurt the plants or trees.

TEST PATTERN

Watch a variety of TV shows for one week. Use this worksheet to keep track of ways TV commercials and programs portray God and the creatures made in his image—people.

1. What *program* most insulted your intelligence?

2. What *commercial* assumed you had the lowest IQ?

3. What was the most unrealistic program you saw all week? Explain.

4. What was the most realistic program you saw all week? Explain.

5. What program seemed to encourage people to make fun of God or Christianity? Explain.

6. What program portrayed God or Christianity in a positive way? Explain.

7. What *commercial* would you nominate the *worst* for making Christians seem to be less than God's best? Explain.

8. What *commercial* would you nominate the *best* for portraying Christians as God's best creation? Explain.

9. What *program* would you nominate the *worst* for making Christians seem to be less than God's best? Explain.

10. What *program* would you nominate the *best* for portraying Christians as God's best creation? Explain.

11. Based on your week of viewing, how well does television portray people as being created in God's image? Explain.

More from Group's Active Bible Curriculum™

Yes, I want scripture-based learning that blasts away boredom.

For Senior High

Quantity			Quantity		
_____	207-2	**Counterfeit Religions** ISBN 1-55945-207-2 $6.95	_____	210-2	**The Joy of Serving** ISBN 1-55945-210-2 $6.95
_____	202-1	**Getting Along With Parents** ISBN 1-55945-202-1 $6.95	_____	205-6	**Knowing God's Will** ISBN 1-55945-205-6 $6.95
_____	208-0	**The Gospel of John: Jesus' Teachings** ISBN 1-55945-208-0 $6.95	_____	209-9	**Making Good Decisions** ISBN 1-55945-209-9 $6.95
_____	200-5	**Hazardous to Your Health** ISBN 1-55945-200-5 $6.95	_____	201-3	**School Struggles** ISBN 1-55945-201-3 $6.95
_____	203-X	**Is Marriage in Your Future?** ISBN 1-55945-203-X $6.95	_____	206-4	**Sex: A Christian Perspective** ISBN 1-55945-206-4 $6.95
_____	211-0	**Jesus' Death & Resurrection** ISBN 1-55945-211-0 $6.95	_____	204-8	**Your Life as a Disciple** ISBN 1-55945-204-8 $6.95

For Junior High/Middle School

Quantity			Quantity		
_____	109-2	**Becoming Responsible** ISBN 1-55945-109-2 $6.95	_____	108-4	**Is God Unfair?** ISBN 1-55945-108-4 $6.95
_____	100-9	**Boosting Self-Esteem** ISBN 1-55945-100-9 $6.95	_____	107-6	**Making Parents Proud** ISBN 1-55945-107-6 $6.95
_____	118-1	**Drugs & Drinking** ISBN 1-55945-118-1 $6.95	_____	103-3	**Peer Pressure** ISBN 1-55945-103-3 $6.95
_____	102-5	**Evil and the Occult** ISBN 1-55945-102-5 $6.95	_____	104-1	**Prayer** ISBN 1-55945-104-1 $6.95
_____	111-4	**Genesis: The Beginning** ISBN 1-55945-111-4 $6.95	_____	101-7	**Today's Music: Good or Bad?** ISBN 1-55945-101-7 $6.95
_____	110-6	**Guys & Girls: Understanding Each Other** ISBN 1-55945-110-6 $6.95	_____	105-X	**What's a Christian?** ISBN 1-55945-105-X $6.95

Yes, please send me _____ of Group's Active Bible Curriculum studies at $6.95 each plus $3 postage and handling per order. Colorado residents add 3% sales tax.

03382

▶ ☐ Check enclosed ☐ VISA ☐ MasterCard

Credit card # _____

Expires _____

(Please print)

Name _____

Address _____

City _____

State _____ ZIP _____

Daytime phone (____) _____

Take this order form or a photocopy to your favorite Christian bookstore. Or mail to:

Group's Active Bible Curriculum
Box 481 ● Loveland, CO 80539 ● (303) 669-3836